ROYAL REVERENCE

Embracing Your Noble Self by Cultivating Self Respect

Rochinda Pickens
The Crown Checker

Royal Reverence
Copyright © 2024 by Rochinda Pickens

All rights reserved. No part of this publication may be reproduced, distributed, or transmitted in any form or by any means, including photocopying, recording or other electronic or mechanical methods, without the prior written permission of the author, except in the case of brief quotations embodied in reviews and certain other non-commercial uses permitted by copyright law.

Without in any way limiting the author's and publisher's exclusive rights under copyright, any use of this publication to "train" generative artificial intelligence (AI) technologies to generate text is expressly prohibited. The author reserves all rights to license uses of this work for generative AI training and development of machine learning language models.

Printed in the United States of America

Paperback ISBN: **978-1-7326832-4-2**
eBook ISBN: **979-8-218-12789-3**

Purpose Publishing LLC.
13194 US Highway 301 South - Suite 417
Riverview, Florida 33578
www.PurposePublishing.com

Dedication

To my amazing Lord and Savior Jesus Christ, thank you for allowing the words throughout this book to manifest in the souls of each reader. I dedicate this book to every woman who has taken the time to adjust, check or correct another sister's crown.

The "crown" we carry is an inheritance that has been given to each of us. An inheritance we must protect and honor daily.

Blessings and Abundance,
~ Rochinda ~

Contents

Introduction 7

Chapter 1: Crown Yourself with Confidence 11

Chapter 2: Set Healthy Boundaries Like a
Queen's Moat 23

Chapter 3: Treat Yourself with the Care a
Queen Gets 35

Chapter 4: Build Your Own Queendom
of Support 47

Chapter 5: Wear Your Crown with Pride 61

Chapter 6: Rule Your Kingdom Through
Self-Acceptance and Growth 77

Chapter 7: Overcoming Obstacles with
Royal Resilience 95

Conclusion: A Closing Note on Royal Reverence ... 111

A Blessing on Your Journey 113

About the Author 115

More from the Author 118

Introduction

Greetings Friends! As The Crown Checker, it's my honor to welcome you into the journey of Royal Reverence. I've served hundreds of women as a life coach, but now I want to spread my message even wider - the message that each one of us deserves to wear our crowns with the utmost pride.

Now, you all may know me as the Crown Checker, but I stand before you not as an expert with all the answers, but as a companion on your journey to self-discovery. I understand the intricate dance of balancing the roles of womanhood, family, business partnerships, motherhood, grandparenthood, and entrepreneurship. It's a dance that requires resilience, self-love, and a recognition of one's own regal essence.

For many years, I, too, struggled to recognize the crown within. The demands of daily life often overshadowed the innate majesty within me. It was through moments of reflection, a commitment to personal growth, and the understanding that imperfections are the jewels that make us unique, is when I began to truly embrace my regal identity.

Throughout the book, I invite you to join me in exploring the various facets of our royal selves. As we delve into the realms of self-identity, imperfections, and the journey toward embracing our inner sovereignty, know that you are not alone. We are on this path together, each of us unveiling our crowns at our own pace.

What exactly does that mean? Well in this book, we'll explore the keys to true confidence through embracing what I call our "inner queendom" or the royalty inside all of us. You'll hear directly from me at the start of every chapter as I lay out my unique perspectives on how to increase feelings of self-worth.

Then in each chapter, we'll dive deeper into specific strategies embracing queen-like principles to build self-respect. You'll get tips for setting healthy boundaries, practicing essential self-care, surrounding yourself with supportive communities, and of course carrying yourself with the dignity of a true queen. Along the journey, I'll share coaching stories and insights into putting these queenly lessons into action.

Finally, we'll end each chapter with a practical exercise so you can immediately apply what you've learned. The Noble Notables will reinforce how concepts relate back to honoring your inner nobility. By the book's end, you'll have the key tools to truly ascend into Royal Reverence!

So, without further ado, turn the page and prepare as we commence embracing queenly wisdom to rule your inner and outer queendom! This journey starts with crowning yourself in confidence.

Chapter 1

Crown Yourself with Confidence

In this sacred space of self-discovery, I, your Crown Checker, warmly welcome you to the journey of unveiling your inner majesty. As a woman, wife, mother, Nana, and fellow business owner, I've walked a path not dissimilar to yours. It took time, trials, and a lot of self-reflection for me to grow into my own queenly qualities. In the chapters that follow, I'll share insights from my personal journey on each regal topic, alongside practical exercises designed to ground these concepts within you.

My fellow Queens and Kings! As the Crown Checker, I'm thrilled we're embarking on our first lesson - crowning yourself in authentic confidence. I can't emphasize enough how foundational true confidence is for self-respect. So, let's explore what I mean by true confidence.

In the quiet corners of my childhood, amidst the echoes of my mother's wisdom, there existed a profound truth that became the cornerstone of my journey—being wonderfully made is an inherent part of our birthright in Christ. My mother, a pillar of strength and wisdom, would often remind me, "If you don't respect yourself, nobody else is going to respect you."

Her words were not just about etiquette or outward appearances; they were about understanding that our actions, words, and demeanor reflected a birthright bestowed upon us by our Creator. It was a legacy that went beyond the temporal confines of familial ties and transcended into a spiritual heritage. "You have to respect yourself," she would emphasize, "and as a woman, you're a lady at all times."

As her daughter, I was entrusted with a responsibility—a representation of the values instilled within our family. The echoes of her guidance lingered in my ears, a constant reminder that someone was always watching, and every step, and every word, had the potential to reach back to her. My mother's teachings were not about conforming to societal norms; they were about embodying a higher truth, a royal reverence for the essence within.

ROYAL REVERENCE

In the realm of self-respect, my mother's influence was omnipresent. From the way I carried myself to the words I spoke, she left an indelible mark on the canvas of my identity. "You better walk in that room with the attitude like you're the stuff," she would say, emphasizing the importance of self-assuredness and dignity.

Yet, beyond the maternal guidance, there was a revelation—an awakening to the deeper understanding of our birthright. In the journey towards self-respect, it dawned on me that the DNA of my birthright was intricately woven into the fabric of my existence. It wasn't about knowing the year and place of my birth; it was about recognizing the divine parentage and acknowledging God as the ultimate Creator.

As I delved deeper into Psalms 139, the scripture resonated with my newfound significance— "We are wonderfully and marvelously made." Our parents may have given birth to us, but they did not create the intricate details of our being. The birthright I speak of goes beyond human lineage; it is a gift from our Heavenly Father, a calling to show up at our best, to radiate love, and to live a life that reflects the inherent marvel of our creation.

In this pursuit of royal reverence, I've come to understand that our birthright is not just a passive inheritance—it is a guiding blueprint. Even in moments of falling short, the blueprint remains, urging us to return to the path of authenticity and divine alignment. For in knowing our birthright, we find the compass that directs us toward a life of purpose, impact, and the true essence of self-respect. As the saying goes, "When you know better, you do better." Maya Angelou. And armed with the understanding of our birthright, we embark on a journey of doing better, honoring the royal reverence within us.

False bravado is when people mask insecurities under claims of confidence. But real royalty doesn't pretend; they radiate confidence from a place of genuine self-worth. Think of the effortless certainty Queen Elizabeth exuded in her right to rule as she reigned over the United Kingdom and other Commonwealth realms until her death in September 2022. We must cultivate that same assuredness in our own abilities before we can ascend as rulers over our queendoms.

So how do we grow real confidence? By identifying our God given talents and honing our God given skills. Pay attention to what activities make you feel alive and capable. Notice when you achieve something, don't dismiss it; celebrate it as proof of your talents. Even small daily victories develop confidence over time. Slowly raise challenges to test yourself in supportive settings. Quiet any inner critic eroding your certainty about self. Surround yourself with encouragers who magnify your strengths.

I've used these principles for years in my confident coaching practice. Clients often say that embracing their "inner queen" mentality was their breakthrough. Like my client Vivian who hated public speaking. By connecting to her visionary queen energy, she now excels at high-stakes presentations. Vivian stopped downplaying her expertise and started proudly sharing her kingdom gifts with the world. And you too can manifest your royalty through confident pursuits!

False bravado is simply a facade - when we pretend to be confident by bragging, putting others down, avoiding vulnerability, or refusing to acknowledge weaknesses. It's all a bluster without substance.

For instance, someone with false confidence might say "I'm the best at everything!" but crumble at the slightest criticism. Or they hide their fears behind arrogant statements rather than risk exposing uncertainties. False confidence is a house of cards requiring constant maintenance to avoid collapse.

Real confidence, however, stands sturdy as a castle against life's storms. It's built slowly but surely through meaningful victories and proving one's abilities over time. By setting small goals outside our comfort zones, and achieving them through challenging work, we construct our confidence. Each goal we conquer further fortifies our self-assurance and builds our confidence.

For example, if public speaking terrifies someone, they start by sharing short ideas at team meetings. As they get comfortable with sharing, they move to local community presentations. Confronting fears builds the resilient confidence to eventually doing keynote speeches.

The key is being honest with oneself. Admit weaknesses and doubts, don't hide them behind bravado. Use fears as clues toward goals for confidence-building. Lean on support systems to reinforce growth rather than shame. And remember - confidence is a lifelong construction project requiring maintenance. But with steady work, we cultivate unshakable faith in our right to rule over our queendoms!

A Royal Conclusion:

As we conclude today's journey into authentic confidence as our royal foundation, remember - true queens display certainty quietly rooted in substance rather than demanding pedestals. Place your crown as a self-evident inner knowing rather than seeking validation from others. Spend time discovering natural talents to boldly enrich your kingdom and being more honest with yourself. The greatest leaders shine by empowering others to do the same.

Practical Exercise:

Now, try this simple but powerful exercise. Make a Crowned with Confidence List of 10 things that bring out your inner queen's gifts. Revisit it whenever you need reminders of your royalty!

Chapter 1 Noble Notable:

True confidence comes from connecting with my authentic strengths and talents and boldly offering them to my queendom. My crown represents the certainty in my sovereign abilities.

It's your turn. How will you apply it? Write down what stuck out and how you'll apply it.

Crowned Confidence List

1.

2.

3.

4.

5.

6.

7.

8.

9.

10.

ROYAL REVERENCE

ROCHINDA PICKENS

ROYAL REVERENCE

Chapter 2

Set Healthy Boundaries Like a Queen's Moat

Greetings fellow rulers! As the Crown Checker, I'm thrilled to guide you in our next lesson on constructing robust boundaries around your domain.

Navigating the delicate terrain of boundaries proved to be a transformative chapter in my journey towards self-respect. As women, we often find ourselves entangled in the intricate dance of people-pleasing, a pattern that drains our energy and leaves us feeling depleted. Setting healthy boundaries emerged as an essential skill—one that contributes significantly to maintaining self-respect and reclaiming our personal power.

I vividly recall a time in my life when the word "no" felt like a foreign concept. Always eager to lend a helping hand, I found myself entangled in a web of commitments that left me overwhelmed and depleted. My disease, as I now refer to it, was people-pleasing—a draining endeavor that had no end.

My mother's teachings echoed in my mind—respect yourself and know your worth. It was time to take those words to heart and establish boundaries that would protect my energy, time, and my self-respect.

Setting boundaries required a paradigm shift, a departure from the relentless "yes" that had become my default response. Learning to say "no" became a practice, a necessary exercise in reclaiming my time and prioritizing my well-being. It was about acknowledging that saying "no" to certain things was, in fact, saying "yes" to myself.

I adopted a strategy of writing down my top priorities for the month—my top three commitments that aligned with my goals, values, and well-being. This preemptive planning served as a powerful tool in gracefully declining additional requests. When someone approached me with an ask, I could confidently respond, "I've already allocated my time this month, perhaps next month would work better."

The journey towards setting boundaries wasn't about shutting doors entirely; it was about timing and prioritization. Saying "not right now" didn't mean a permanent "no"; it was an acknowledgment of my limits and a commitment to honor the promises I had made to myself.

For those who find it challenging to establish and enforce personal boundaries, my advice would be to start small. Begin by practicing saying "no" in low-stakes situations and gradually build up to more significant commitments. Write down your priorities, create a roadmap for your time, and communicate your boundaries in advance. Remember, setting boundaries isn't about being inflexible; it's about creating space for self-respect and ensuring that your energy is spent on endeavors that align with your purpose.

As you navigate the delicate dance of boundaries, keep in mind that it's a journey of self-discovery and empowerment. Embrace the art of saying "no" with grace, and in doing so, you'll find that establishing healthy boundaries becomes a cornerstone in your pursuit of royal reverence and self-respect.

A queen's authority depends greatly on maintaining secure borders around her queendom. Without clear delineations of who may enter and the terms of access, a kingdom falls into chaos making the job of ruling nearly impossible.

It's the same in managing our inner sovereignty. Healthy boundaries are essential for self-respect by protecting our peace, priorities, and principles. When boundaries are ambiguous or porous, we exhaust ourselves trying to manage unrelenting demands from others. Our energy drainage leaves little for effectively governing our queendom.

Therefore, we must create explicit boundaries much like a moat circumscribing a castle. This means identifying what requests or behaviors we will entertain versus which we unequivocally reject. Then clearly communicating those standards along with proportional consequences.

For instance, proclaim to a pushy friend that while advice is welcome, unsolicited criticism will result in less access to you. If they violate that boundary with judgements, gradually limit interactions for a set period. Hold the line until they respect the moat!

Now let's dive deeper into boundary setting strategies and examples...

By chapter's end, revisit your standards and shore up any weak spots in your moat. Protecting your queendom starts with you!

Here are some tips on setting healthy boundaries in different contexts:

At Home:

- Communicate needs for personal space/quiet time to family. Set house rules allowing you to retreat to a "throne room" alone when required.
- Schedule focused quality time with kids. When available, give them full loving attention and be fully present. If not, kindly enforce limits.
- Clarify chore expectations and consequences for family members not upholding duties to the household queendom. Follow through consistently.

At Work:

- Make workload/hours limitations clear from the outset of any new role. If overburdened, respectfully speak up about what you can realistically manage.
- Institute communication boundaries by not responding to emails/calls outside defined work times except for pre-agreed urgent matters.
- Don't take on unofficial roles/requests without assessing if they fit your sovereign priorities before agreeing. Practice saying no.

In Business:

- Clearly state policies on payments, returns, service scope etc. so customers understand terms for working with your queendom.
- Create email/contact forms to allow efficient customer communication while filtering out those wanting preferential treatment.
- Build referral networks so you can suggest other "kingdoms" when requests don't suit your business' boundaries.

In Ministry:

- Tell your congregation upfront when you are available for guidance vs times set aside for self-care. Keep days off sacrosanct.
- Define scope of counseling - for general talks make appointments. For emergencies share crisis resources too.
- Kindly avoid getting entangled in church politics/conflicts. Redirect members to focus on collective faith goals over divisions.

The key in every domain is first knowing your limits. Then transparently expressing them while redirecting people to respect your sovereign queendom's borders! What boundaries will you instill?

A Royal Conclusion:

As we part today having explored boundary setting for our peace of mind, recall that limits honestly expressed never diminish your light. They illuminate exactly where your light ends, allowing others' own brilliance room to breathe rather than enabling those who would eclipse your shine. Borders teach respect. And self-respect starts by accepting nothing less from words, actions and spirits allowed access to your grace. Now rule serenely over the garden of your heart!

Practical Exercise:

Over the next week, choose one major area of your life to focus on setting better boundaries.

Step 1: Map out what current boundaries exist, if any. How are people made aware of them? How consistently are they enforced?

Step 2: Based on problems you face, brainstorm 2-3 priority boundaries to put in place around requests, communications, behaviors etc.

Step 3: Create a specific communication plan for expressing the new boundaries. Ensure clarity on exactly what the boundaries are, how they will be enforced, and consequences for violations.

Step 4: Begin informing key people of the new boundaries either directly or by posting them prominently as "queen's decrees." Reiterate them politely when people test them.

Step 5: After 1-2 weeks of consistently upholding the boundary, evaluate effectiveness. Adjust and expand to other areas as needed.

Reclaiming sovereignty over your queendom starts with moat building! Protect your peace and priorities.

Chapter 2 Noble Notable:

Healthy boundaries clearly communicate and uphold my standards of how I allow people to interact within my queendom. Just like a queen's moat shielding her castle, boundaries are essential for self-respect.

ROYAL REVERENCE

It's your turn. How will you apply it? Write down what stuck out and how you'll apply it.

Top Monthly Priorities and Commitments

1.

2.

3.

4.

5.

6.

7.

8.

9.

10.

ROCHINDA PICKENS

ROYAL REVERENCE

ROCHINDA PICKENS

Chapter 3

Treat Yourself with the Care a Queen Gets

Greetings my esteemed rulers! As your Crown Checker, I'm excited for this lesson on one of the greatest yet most neglected keys to self-respect - lavishing yourself with royal treatment.

In the royal tapestry of life, there exists a profound truth—a queen is not only adorned and cared for by others; she also knows how to treat herself like the royalty she is. As I reflect on this, I am reminded of a personal revelation—one that shifted my perspective from seeking external care to realizing the immense power of self-care.

In our society, there's often an underlying expectation that others should cater to our needs. It's a mindset that permeates relationships, leaving us waiting for someone else to fulfill our desires and treat us with the care we deserve. Just yesterday, in a candid video with my husband, Alan, as he fixed a drawer, I declared my intention for 2024—to start asking for what I want. It wasn't about entitlement; it was about recognizing the power of articulating my needs.

In the past, I grappled with the notion that if someone couldn't intuitively understand my desires, then what purpose did they serve in my life? It was a flawed mindset that placed the responsibility of my happiness on external factors or other people. However, a newfound understanding emerged—that my ability to care for myself was more pivotal than waiting for others to do it for me.

Taking care of yourself is an act of self-love, a declaration that you value your well-being and deserve to be treated with the utmost care and attention. It's about recognizing that you are the sovereign of your life, and your actions should reflect the respect and admiration you hold for yourself.

I recall a moment of realization when I understood the importance of asking for what I want. It wasn't a demand; it was a self-affirmation—an acknowledgment that my needs mattered and were worthy of expression. Learning to communicate my desires with grace allowed me to take control of my narrative and actively participate in my own care.

As a queen in my own life, I've discovered the significance of treating myself with the same reverence I might expect from others. It goes beyond pampering or indulgence; it's about understanding that my well-being is my responsibility. From self-care rituals to pursuing passions, I've learned that the true essence of royalty lies in the ability to nurture and uplift oneself.

So, to those navigating the intricate dance of self-care, my advice is—don't wait for others to treat you like royalty; start by treating yourself like the queen you are. Embrace the power of self-love, honor your desires, and actively engage in the rituals and activities that bring joy and fulfillment. Remember, you have the regal authority to create a life where every act of self-care is a testament to your worth and the respect you hold for the sovereign within.

Consider how a queen's needs are catered to without question. Servants ensure nutritious meals reach her table daily. Her baths are drawn at optimum temperature and filled with the finest oils. The queen sleeps undisturbed on silken sheets. Her closest advisors know that a rested, well-fed queen governs most effectively.

Yet we commoners resist similar self-care, feeling undeserving, guilty, or lacking time. We run ourselves ragged trying to rule kingdoms with depleted energy. But how can we expect our subjects to treat us like royalty if we do not first crown ourselves with care?

Prioritizing Self-Care

Queens rightfully dedicate large parts of their day to personal wellness - anything less diminishes their competence. Likewise, we must make self-care an utmost priority instead of the last resort. Block off time for healthy routines that refuel you. Never apologize or feel selfish for needing renewal - crowns should not tarnish due to fatigue!

Practice saying no to extra duties infringing upon that carved-out time. Treat meals with leisure rather than as an afterthought. Approach sleep as non-negotiable. Recruit family members as your royal support system if needed, asking them to uphold your self-care time from disturbances. Simply remind them - "a queen governs best when her needs come first!"

Now let's cover specific self-care strategies and specific tips fit for a queen:

Healthy Eating

- Plan weekly menus that nourish you - fresh vegetables/fruits, lean proteins, whole grains, healthy fats

- Cook batch meals, when possible, to have quick royal feasts ready and prepped.
- Hydrate constantly with pure water or herbal teas in a gem-encrusted goblet
- Treat yourself to premium ingredients - spices, quality oils, exotic dishes

Soothing Self-Massage

- Draw candlelit aromatherapy baths with Himalayan or Epsom soaks
- Experiment with essential oil blends to ease stress
- Apply luxurious lotions after bathing while massaging tension away
- Get professional massages monthly to melt physical/mental strain

Rest & Relaxation

- Prioritize 8+ hours of sleep nightly. Block out noise, light, and obligations infringing on precious rest!
- Allow time to lounge on plush chaise reading, listening to music, contemplating life.
- Take power naps when exhausted - even 15 minutes can revive a fatigued ruler.
- Say no to anything depleting reserves, so you can refuel adequately.

The key is recognizing relaxation, joy, and pleasure are essential to rule well rather than frivolous extravagances. You deserve rejuvenation! What self-care will you schedule first? Self-care is not merely about superficial pampering but replenishing us deeply so we can serve our kingdoms better. Let's explore the external and internal benefits:

Healthy Eating

When we nourish ourselves with natural, fresh foods it shows self-respect by demonstrating our body deserves quality fuel. But it also keeps your mind sharper, immunity stronger, skin glowing from within - you emanate royalty from the inside out.

Soothing Self-Massage

Taking time to destress and loosen physical tension proves your whole being deserves care. But it also clears mental fog, lowers anxiety and blood pressure, releases pleasure hormones that combat inflammation - you rule with grace instead of stress-triggered reactions.

Rest & Relaxation

Prioritizing sleep, leisure time, joy activities demonstrate your inner queen knows to recharge fully. But in doing so concentration heightens, patience and playfulness increase, and suddenly creative breakthrough solutions come effortlessly to once stubborn problems!

In summary, self-care represents loving yourself enough to let your light shine at its brightest - for when our cup runneth over, we inevitably enrich our queendoms! Consider how to expand both the external pampering and internal renewal. You deserve nothing less!

A Royal Conclusion:

Dear rulers, may today's lesson settle gently around you - that self-care forms the bedrock for every kingdom, as no ministry can nourish spaces starved of revitalizing nutrients first. Drain yourself dry and little remains to feed the queendom. Rather replenish regularly from fountains filling your cup. Do so not from vain extravagance but aligned to highest stewardship through mindfully meeting holistic needs. Rule over valleys ever verdant!

Practical Exercise:

Over the next two weeks, choose 3 self-care activities to elevate into royal treatments:

1. Enrich

2. eating or drinking routine - try a new healthy, premium ingredient. Dine by candlelight. Use your finest stemware!

3. Gift yourself a soothing experience - take an immersive bubble bath or schedule a massage. Create a relaxing environment. Repeat weekly.

4. Dedicate non-negotiable time to a stress-relieving activity - lounge with a book, listen to a podcast while coloring intricate designs. Remove distractions.

At the end of the fortnight evaluate any positive impacts from this intentional self-care. Explore which if any to sustain long-term. You deserve to rule feeling refreshed!

Chapter 3 Noble Notable:

Treating myself to restorative self-care as consistently as a Queen nourished by her attendants proves my inner royalty. It replenishes me to serve my queendom at my highest capacity. My light shines brightest when my cup runneth over!

ROYAL REVERENCE

It's your turn. How will you apply it? Write down what stuck out and how you'll apply it.

Self Care Goals

1.

2.

3.

4.

5.

6.

7.

8.

9.

10.

ROCHINDA PICKENS

ROYAL REVERENCE

ROCHINDA PICKENS

Chapter 4

Build Your Own Queendom of Support

My worthy sovereigns! As the Crown Checker, I'm thrilled we're discussing a topic integral to self-respect - curating a queendom of supporters who see and celebrate your true worth.

In the tapestry of our lives, the strength and resilience we embody are often intricately woven into the fabric of our supportive community. A pivotal moment that underscored this truth for me occurred during the Kept Woman of God conference. My dear friend, Michelle Gines, eloquently closed out her talk by shedding light on the concept of the six people who eventually carry us out of this life—the pallbearers.

However, Michelle urged each woman in attendance to consider a separate set of individuals—the six sisters carrying them through their current journey. These are not just friends, confidantes, or prayer partners; these are the pillars of support, the ones who go beyond the surface and stand by you through thick and thin. As she spoke, it sparked a reflective moment for many, a soul-searching contemplation about the genuine connections that define our lives.

It is crucial to surround ourselves with a support community that transcends the superficial. These are not merely lunch mates or Facebook friends; they are the devoted friends you can count on and call upon when times get tough. The ones who uplift your spirit, share in your joys, and lend a compassionate ear during moments of vulnerability.

In building your support community, consider not just those who carry you forward but also those who might inadvertently rob you of joy or distract you from your dreams. This discernment is crucial, as it allows you to see people for who they truly are and position them in the rightful places in your life.

The concept of pallbearers is a poignant reminder that life is a collective journey, and we need a tribe that stands beside us in celebration and solace. These are the individuals who celebrate your victories as if they were their own, who share in your defeats with empathy, and who contribute to the symphony of your life with their unwavering presence.

As you reflect on your support community, consider the roles each person plays and the impact they have on your journey. Nurture relationships that add value, inspire growth, and align with the vision you have for your life. In doing so, you cultivate a powerful network that propels you forward and provides the fortitude to face the challenges that may arise.

Remember, the people you choose to surround yourself with are not just observers; they are active participants in the chapters of your life story. Choose wisely and let your support community be a testament to the strength, love, and camaraderie that defines the essence of a life well-lived. So, I want to touch on the rules of your royal community.

Rule #1 – banish the jesters! We all attract naysayers who mask criticism and contempt as "constructive feedback." But faithful friends uplift you even while delivering hard truths with love. So weed out any relational weeds choking your light. Politely minimize contact with those leaving you diminished.

Next, expand your court with cohorts who champion your goals. Identify righteous crusaders for your causes - volunteer teams, mastermind groups, tribes who rally around shared values. Meet regularly to brainstorm progress. Let them hold you accountable to decrees so you manifest them!

Finally, align with partners equally yoked in ambition and self-care. Relationships should amplify both ruler's highest selves, not leave you overwhelmed managing another's kingdom. Frequently ask - does this person nourish or deplete me? Upgrade accordingly!

In summary, self-respect requires removing critics and adding cheerleaders. Surround your throne only with those ensuring your crown stays lifted high! Let's dive deeper into doing exactly that...

Here are some more details on curating a supportive community as royalty would:

Banish the Jesters - Be extremely selective about who you give access to your court and circle of influence. Look for patterns of putting others down, stealing joy, or projecting insecurities. Do they gossip, compare unfairly, constantly play devil's advocate? Ask directly for supportive behavior change, and if it's not consistently provided, gradually remove them from your inner circle.

Expand Your Court - Make a list of causes you feel passionately about whether social justice, arts, faith community, health movement etc. Seek out local chapters/meetups or online forums to join. Contribute actively by sharing your skills. Allow others to hold you accountable for growth goals. Over time, meaningful friendships with fellow changemakers will develop.

Align with Equals - Rather than pursuing any relationship out of scarcity, ask yourself first if this person demonstrates self-awareness/care for their own growth. Do they take responsibility or play victim? Uplifting others versus unhealthy competition? Have integrity between values and actions? Look for consistent embodiment of royalty - self-respect attracts the same. Stay true to standards, don't compromise yourself for the company. Prioritize solitude with dignity, over toxic ties!

The key is realizing supportive community directly correlates to how we inwardly cultivate self-respect. Take relationship building to new heights by curating shared values and missions. Surround yourself only with champions!

Seeking romantic partnerships with those equally committed to personal growth and self-care is key.

The first step is to take an honest inventory of your own journey - your relationship with yourself sets the foundation. Are you actively expanding self-awareness with practices like journaling, meditation, or counseling? Do you set healthy boundaries and uphold them unapologetically? Have you created routines nourishing your whole being - physical, mental, emotional, spiritual? Become the type of royalty you seek first.

From there, vet potential suitors thoroughly. Have candid conversations early about their personal growth path. Ask questions like:

- What daily/weekly self-care routines do you honor consistently?
- How do you deal with conflicts - do you self-reflect before blaming others?
- What boundaries do you set in relationships and why are they important?
- In what ways are you actively working to better yourself?

Listen closely for self-awareness, accountability, and commitment to continual betterment. Warning signs include deflecting questions, vague answers about improving "someday," or statements like "my partner will fix me." Make alignment around self-work and worth a non-negotiable.

Finally, once dating pay close attention to consistency between your partner's words and actions. Do they become codependent and enmeshed or respect your autonomy? Hold you back from goals out of their own insecurity? The right partner expands your opportunities for joyful co-rule, and never diminishes your light. Never compromise your standards for royalty!

Assessing whether a relationship uplifts or drains you and being willing to make tough changes based on that feedback, is key.

Start by checking in with yourself regularly about how you feel after interactions with a given person. Do you leave feeling energized, inspired, cared for and seen? Or are you drained, unhappy, resentful of compromised boundaries or constantly giving without reciprocation?

Don't ignore red flags based on surface chemistry. True soulmate connections still fill your cup. If you consistently feel depleted, have open conversations about what each of you need to feel loved and supported.

If your core emotional needs go unmet for prolonged periods, be willing to loosen attachments rather than waste years waiting for a change. People's capacity to meet your needs depends on their own self-work. You can't do it for them.

Upgrading relationships requires courage and discernment. But the personal growth that comes from recognizing what you deserve, finding the voice to stand unwaveringly for it, and opening space for more mutual connections makes it all worthwhile. Surround yourself only with royalty who makes you feel like the queen or king you are!

A Royal Conclusion:

As we conclude today's journey into intentionally curating community, remember that change begins from within. First unveil and honor the royalty within through self-acceptance, then lovingly allow that dignity to magnetize outer spheres holding equitable reverence. No longer dismiss poor treatment, rather release those unwilling to grow in lockstep devotion into fate's hands with blessing not bitterness. Stay open and a victorious tribe will soon surround your throne!

Practical Exercise:

Over the next month, curate your inner circle using these steps:

1. Identify 1-2 "jesters" draining your energy. Distance yourself from them. Replace time spent with nurturing activities.

2. Seek out one new group aligned with a passionate cause of yours. Attend meet-

ings, share your gifts. Aim for authentic connections.

3. Have an honest conversation with your romantic partner (or evaluate prospects if single) about self-care/growth compatibility using questions provided in this chapter.

4. Assess the overall energy shift in your circle after taking these steps. Feel the lightness of releasing people-pleasing and making space for mutual upliftment!

Chapter 4 Noble Notable:

I manifest supportive community by first committing to my own royalty, then curating my inner circle and relationships around shared values with those who nurture my highest self. I thrive by surrounding my throne only with champions!

It's your turn. How will you apply it? Write down what stuck out and how you'll apply it.

List Jesters:

1.

2.

3.

4.

5.

6.

7.

8.

9.

10.

List Community of Champions:

1.

2.

3.

4.

5.

6.

7.

8.

9.

10.

ROCHINDA PICKENS

ROYAL REVERENCE

ROCHINDA PICKENS

Chapter 5

Wear Your Crown with Pride

My crowned community! As your Crown Checker, I'm overjoyed we've reached another lesson - elevating into the full majesty of supreme self-respect by wearing your crowns with utmost pride and confidence!

Mirror, mirror on the wall, who is that standing tall? As we step into the morning light, beyond our prayers, beyond the daily rituals, there lies a powerful moment of self-affirmation. The mirror in the bathroom becomes a canvas where we paint our self-worth and declare our identity.

For me, the mirror is a constant companion, not just reflecting physical appearances but echoing the sentiments of my soul. "Mirror, mirror on the wall, return to you wonderful, return to you strong, return to you resilient, return to you healed." These words, spoken to my own reflection, are a daily affirmation, a ritual of self-love and empowerment.

In the enchanted tales of our childhood, characters like Cinderella spoke to the mirror, seeking validation of their beauty. Yet, in our reality, the mirror reflects more than just appearances; it mirrors our inner dialogue. How we speak to ourselves in those vulnerable moments sets the tone for the day ahead.

Regardless of the tired eyes, the morning disarray, or the absence of makeup, the mirror becomes a portal to self-respect. "Look at yourself," I whisper, acknowledging the wonderfully made creation staring back at me. It's a reminder that my value is not contingent on external adornments but is intrinsic to my being.

In the narrative of Cinderella, the wicked stepmother sought validation from the mirror, asking, "Who is the fairest one of all?" The mirror, unfailingly honest, proclaimed Cinderella's beauty. In our own stories, the mirror reflects our truth, revealing the authenticity and beauty we carry within.

Affirmations become a shield against the onslaught of negative self-talk that can permeate our minds. Speaking words of healing, resilience, and strength is a deliberate act of self-care. The mirror becomes a sacred space for self-respect, an altar where we honor the divine image in which we were created.

As women, our mindset is our crown, and how we think about ourselves is crucial. If we don't respect ourselves, if we don't affirm our worth, we risk wandering through the day without purpose or direction. The mirror, an honest confidant, reflects not just our physical form but the essence of our self-perception.

So, as you face your reflection each morning, remember the power you hold in speaking words of love and affirmation to yourself. Wear your crown with pride, for you are wonderfully made, a reflection of divine artistry. The mirror is not just a reflection; it is a canvas where you paint the narrative of self-respect, one empowering word at a time.

As in previous chapters, we've been equipped to construct an impenetrable queendom from within. We cultivated true confidence not cockiness, moats of healthy boundaries, courts of support, and most importantly relentless self-care.

Now we are taking another, yet challenging step - publicly owning these well-earned crowns as our divine birthright without apology! No more hiding royal qualities or diminishing accomplishments. If you've done the inward work, display your magnificence for all to see!

Where we once said, "I'm sorry to bother you, but could you..." we now proclaim "As your Queen, my need is X. How may I request your support?" It's time for unashamed advocacy for ourselves!

Where we once undercharged for precious skills, we now declare "My offerings carry supreme value of XYZ based on their transformation power in my queendom." Your price is an unabashed embodiment of your worth!

Where we once silently endured dismissiveness, we now proclaim "I recognize fully my sovereignty, divinity and capability to rule my domain, regardless of any perceptions otherwise." Unflinching self-validation!

Now, let's get into specifics on boldly wearing crowns over hiding them...

A few specifics on proudly owning our worth:

- Make requests and state needs from a place of dignity rather than diminishing your entitlement to having them met. "As royalty deserving care, this is what I require to feel safe/nourished/respected."

- When receiving compliments, simply say thank you rather than deflecting praise.

Don't justify why a skill isn't special. Let it land.

- If undervalued, research fair compensation rates for your expertise. Then transparently convey that rate backed by how you deliver 10x the transformation.

- When facing criticism, pause first for thoughtful response rather than quick emotion. Filter feedback. What resonates as an insight to integrate vs simply projected judgment you can dismiss? Release the latter from your mind.

- Share achievements publicly rather than hiding accomplishments. Making victories visible inspires others in their growth. Humble pride raises all!

Essentially, self-respect means accepting fully both inner light and shadow without denial or inflation. That allows wearing royal qualities boldly but also gives grace for ongoing progress. We never arrive, but continually unfold majesty! What #crownproud declarations will you boldly make?

Owning our radiance with humility is hugely impactful.

It first builds self-intimacy to accept ourselves wholly - the parts we admire and those we judge. We stop chasing validation when we provide unconditional positive regard inwardly, and it stabilizes our self-worth.

Next, it makes space for others' light too. Confidence grounded in truth has no need to compete, control or dim another's sparkle. I shine brighter by freely highlighting colleagues' talents without worrying if my contributions will be overlooked.

There's also power in revealing our truest, most vulnerable self. The world splits into those inspired by our wholeness versus those feeling threatened by our greatness. Freedom comes when we detach from validation or when we seek others validation.

Essentially when self-worth stabilizes, we uplift community. Our light magnetizes those also committed to growth, to building circles of care. Shared vulnerability builds connection with others.

So, wear crowns proudly but gently - with compassion for the journey, not rigid perfectionism. Humble confidence and radical self-acceptance lift all boats! What does accepting your wholeness look like?

You're absolutely right - living with humble confidence and self-acceptance is a lifelong journey that requires ongoing grace and compassion. Rome wasn't built in a day, and neither is realizing one's royalty!

It takes time and repetitive practice to unravel our conditioning around diminishing our light. There will be inevitable setbacks as we retract to old habits of hiding, denying praise, or beating ourselves up harshly. Progress isn't linear.

During those moments, meet yourself gently rather than with shame that feeds the cycle of uncertainty about oneself. Say kind things like, "It's understandable. This vulnerability feels scary as I unwind old patterns that have kept me small. But there's no rush here. Let me try again."

Give space too for low days when impostor syndrome, feeling like a fraud despite success, inevitably rears its head. If we inflate self-perception, ego arises which masks deep insecurities. It's healthy to sometimes feel unremarkable too! Those days remind us royalty has nothing to do with achievements - it's our birthright.

Overall, focus less on some imaginary finish line and instead enjoy the journey of shedding former limitations. Expect difficulties while building trust in your capability to manage both. Each moment you show up boldly yet compassionately is a triumph! Consistency compounds over years form unshakable self-respect. I'm here cheering you on each imperfect step ahead!

A Royal Conclusion:

My queens, take with you from today's final teaching the life-changing revelation that crowns should sparkle boldly atop heads held high, never tucked away carelessly in shameful shadows. Our regalia shines, but brightly broadcasting victory won through incrementally actualizing our noblest selves, not when it's flashy or even dull. So, stand tall in your becoming ruler! Radiance awaits just ahead...

Practical Exercise:

Over the next month, strengthen wearing your crown proudly through these habits:

1. Write down 3 accomplishments from the week before in a "Royal Victories" journal. Add to it weekly. Re-read when you need confidence boosts.

2. When someone compliments you, practice simply saying "Thank you, I appreciate you noticing" without deflection or downplaying the compliment.

3. Make at least 1 bold "crown proud" proclamation verbally each day - stating your needs, talents, values. Start small!

4. When you catch yourself hiding accomplishments or needs out of unworthiness, gently pivot: "As a child of the Creator, fully worthy of care, I deserve to take up space and express my sovereignty."

Chapter 5 Noble Notable:

I honor my crowned royalty by boldly yet compassionately owning my worth and achievements without concealing them. For hiding my light would deprive my queendom and community of my brightest leadership. I proudly wear my crown as my sovereign birthright!

It's your turn. How will you apply it? Write down what stuck out and how you'll apply it.

List Royal Victories:

1.

2.

3.

4.

5.

6.

7.

8.

9.

10.

ROYAL REVERENCE

List Crown Proud Victories:

1.

2.

3.

4.

5.

6.

7.

8.

9.

10.

List Mirror Affirmations:

1.

2.

3.

4.

5.

6.

7.

8.

9.

10.

ROYAL REVERENCE

ROCHINDA PICKENS

ROYAL REVERENCE

Chapter 6

Rule Your Kingdom Through Self-Acceptance and Growth

Greetings, my cherished monarchs! As your Crown Checker, before we conclude our journey, I want to share wisdom that takes most by surprise - the path to self-mastery requires embracing where we stand today as much as striving for tomorrow. Aligning self-acceptance and improvement unlocks our highest sovereignty.

In the grand tapestry of personal development and self-discovery, there's a delicate dance between the pursuit of personal growth and the embrace of self-acceptance. It's a dance I've known well, one that traverses the realms of continuous improvement while recognizing the intrinsic value and worth within.

I am an ardent advocate for personal growth, and an enthusiast of self-development. The belief in the adage that the biggest room is the room for improvement has been a guiding force in my journey. Yet, nestled within this pursuit lies the nuanced challenge of self-acceptance—a realization that sometimes eludes those caught in the perpetual quest for becoming better.

The paradox emerges—how do we balance the desire for improvement with the fundamental need for self-acceptance? The journey begins with a profound acknowledgment: you are valuable, wonderfully made, and deserving of love and acceptance just as you are. It's a transformative revelation that shifts the focus from external validation to an internal sense of worth.

For those who struggle with never feeling enough or worthy, the first step is to arrive at a place where you genuinely like yourself. The danger lies in constantly seeking approval from others, tethering your self-worth to external validations. I vividly recall years when my actions were fueled by the need to be accepted, to be recognized by others. It wasn't until I embraced the truth—I am enough—that my perspective shifted.

ROYAL REVERENCE

Knowing who you are and acknowledging your worthiness independent of external opinions is a pivotal moment. It liberates you from the shackles of perpetual people-pleasing and allows you to stand firm in the authenticity of your being. Rejections or exclusions no longer serve as disqualifications but rather as redirections towards spaces that align with your true self.

However, self-acceptance doesn't negate the importance of personal growth and improvement. The distinction lies in the motivation behind these endeavors. Improvement should stem from a desire to enhance your skills, knowledge, and well-being for your own fulfillment, not to gain external validation.

So, as we navigate the dance of self-acceptance and personal growth, let's remember that the journey involves two intertwining steps. Embrace the beautiful truth—I am enough. Simultaneously, fuel the flame of personal growth, not for the approval of others, but for the enrichment of your own journey. In this delicate dance, find the harmony that allows you to grow into the best version of yourself while cherishing the extraordinary essence that you already are.

Consider gardeners tending spring seeds with care to bloom in season, not demanding instant maturity. We must nurture gradual evolution too, not judge current progress harshly.

So how do we accept ourselves without stagnation? By practicing self-compassion as our foundation while setting intentions invitations upward, not rigid demands. Here are the keys:

Accept Where You Are Now

The first secret is recognizing every queen rules over a kingdom in some phase of expansion or repair at any given time. Your territory has both flowing springs and patches requiring stewardship. This is growth - not fixed, perfect bliss.

Our self-talk must honor the maturity present now, not focus on missing pieces. Does your queendom need more structural support? Perhaps it does, and it already contains gorgeous gems that can be appreciated. Talk to yourself as a beloved child, not stern a taskmaster.

Cultivate intentions instead of demands, envisioning your best while respecting natural timing. Growth cannot be forced, only nurtured patiently through consistent care as seasons change. Where are you now? What intentions guide next steps?

Set Evolving Intentions

Clarify your sovereign priorities before declaring royal decrees over your queendom. What would raise your collective consciousness and empowerment to new heights? Set intentions around that north star.

Better work-life balance allows more community service? Or, will conversations on taboo topics open minds? Maybe passing on cultural traditions will enrich your family?

Intentions feel energizing as they meet us where we are for who we are, not some fictional ideal. They invite rather than demand. And as ruler, you hold the right to modify intentions fluidly based on recalibrations of your highest good.

Stay present and discerning - know when to course correct to avoid overly rigid goals or sabotaging real progress. Trust your maturing intuition.

Approve of Yourself and Your Queendom

Finally, talk to yourself daily like you admire a promising heir to the throne. Note the effort made in the right direction with compassion no matter the outcome. Did your communication improve slightly? Did you speak out once despite fear? Acknowledge that courage!

Write loving notes of growth witnessed like a nurturing mentor strengthened by seeing your development. Become your own best encourager. This quiets the inner critic keeping you small and clears space for wisdom.

Soon you'll witness gradual transformation through self-acceptance to activate higher motivation. Water these seeds and watch yourself bloom.

In closing, reflect on how to balance self-approval with evolving dreams. Patience with the process allows magic! We need to dive deeper into why self-acceptance creates fertile soil for growth rather than complacency.

Self-acceptance provides a nurturing environment to take risks, fail, and try again without self-judgment interfering. Think of a bed of soft moss trying to grow on harsh pavement. The falling leaves quickly decompose back into nutrients for new buds. The latter bruises any seedlings.

When we accept exactly where we are, we stop wasting energy beating ourselves up over not being farther along or because progress feels slow. We can channel that energy directly into the next nourishing action despite imperfections. The moss remains below to break any falls.

Self-acceptance also quiets the inner critic's constant flood of shame, doubt, or deflation around efforts so we can hear our inner wisdom. That calm inner voice - not distorted by past wounds - channels creative ideas for next steps and discerns highest priorities aligned to meaning. We can access clearer guidance.

Essentially, radical self-acceptance creates space free from constant judgement for new growth to emerge in each season. We look honestly at what fertilization the garden needs now without self-blame for any bare patches. Then we cultivate patiently, rooted in compassion for the process. This is the path to blossom as our boldest, brightest selves in time!

Setting evolving intentions is a more flexible, compassionate alternative to rigid goals. Here is a deeper explanation:

Goals often root us in the mindset that we are fundamentally lacking in some way currently. They focus on some end destination making us think we will only be worthy/happy/successful after arriving there. Goals create separation from the now.

Intentions on the other hand start by appreciating who we are and what strengths we have developed on the journey so far. Think - "I accept my emotional intelligence strengths while also holding an intention to keep expanding empathy and listening skills over my lifetime."

An intention feels like a current flowing in a life-affirming direction rather than a static bullseye we beat ourselves up for missing. We get curious about possibilities while respecting organic timing.

Intentions evolve flexibly to redirect wherever your soul guides rather than rigidly sticking to what ego once thought would satisfy. Maybe you realize financial targets cared for the wrong priorities. You pivot efforts to more meaningful work.

Setting intentions involves regular check-ins with yourself. "Does this still energize and align to my core values?" Modify based on intuition and growth. Remove self-judgment about "failed" goals along the way.

Simply nurture the soil and let the seedling determine in season what form brings greatest joy. The key is consistency in caring - not perfection.

Self-Approving Thoughts:

- Celebrating small daily efforts and progress rather than focusing on shortcomings
- Using encouraging inner dialogue emphasizing "I am enough"
- Avoiding comparison with others to determine self-worth
- Seeing missteps as opportunities to adjust gracefully rather than personal failings

Self-Approving Actions:

- Speaking up about personal needs and boundaries rather than suppressing them
- Pursuing activities that spark joy and align with values for YOU, not just duties
- Making space to nourish physical/emotional/spiritual health
- Owning strengths and accomplishments rather than downplaying gifts

Overall Mood:

- Feeling empowered and at peace to let go of control
- Exuding quiet confidence balanced with humility
- Holding head high during adversity while acknowledging vulnerability
- Emanating passion for long-term goals fused with contentment now

The key is balancing self-love with self-responsibility. Know you are ENOUGH while also evolving. Check in often: How do I feel about and treat myself lately? Am I my own best friend? If not, get curious why with compassion not judgment.

A Royal Conclusion:

As we integrate these lessons on balancing self-love and forward movement, remember progress flows in seasons rather than linear timelines. Some periods will bring leaps of exponential growth when we feel in flow alignment. Others require resting in fallow soil while strengthening roots unseen for the next bloom. Both bring vital purpose. Meet yourself exactly where you stand today with nurturing acceptance, while planting seeds of intention for who you're becoming with gentle encouragement. The rest unfolds in divine timing.

Practical Exercise:

Over the next month, strengthen self-acceptance while inviting growth through these steps:

1. Each morning, write down 3 acceptance-based affirmations about your inherent worth, talents etc.

2. Identify 1-2 fluid intentions to nourish rather than rigid goals with deadlines. Check if they align to joy.

3. Make time to simply notice areas you judge yourself for. Then consciously release judgment and get curious about the roots behind behaviors with compassion.

4. Whenever progress feels slow or inspiration lacks, avoid criticism. Instead thank yourself for continuing to turn up with patience repeatedly.

Chapter 6 Noble Notable:

I nurture my highest sovereignty by practicing unconditional self-acceptance while cultivating flexible intentions for joyful expansion. This empowers my unique rhythm of blossoming over forcible change. My inner light grows brightly through compassionate patience with myself.

It's your turn. How will you apply it? Write down what stuck out and how you'll apply it.

Royalty Goals

1.

2.

3.

4.

5.

6.

7.

8.

9.

10.

ROYAL REVERENCE

11.

12.

13.

14.

15.

16.

17.

18.

19.

20.

Areas Where I Will Speak Up

1.

2.

3.

4.

5.

6.

7.

8.

9.

10.

ROYAL REVERENCE

ROCHINDA PICKENS

ROYAL REVERENCE

Chapter 7

Overcoming Obstacles with Royal Resilience

My cherished rulers! As the Crown Checker, I come with a special message today on life's greatest illusion - that queens effortlessly glide from success to success without ever facing storms. Quite the contrary! Every queen worth her salt has proven resilience by overcoming mighty obstacles blocking her ascent.

Life, like a captivating novel, unfolds with unpredictable twists and turns. I, too, have had those moments—challenges that demanded more than just resilience, obstacles that tested the very core of my being. Yet, in the face of adversity, I've learned to navigate a path of triumph and growth, for the obstacles that once seemed insurmountable have become steppingstones toward a more profound understanding of self.

A dear friend once shared a profound piece of wisdom with me. She said, "Everything that the Lord has been doing in your life over these years, don't you dare allow a low crack to let somebody slide right in and tear down everything that God has done." Those words became a beacon of accountability, a reminder that amidst the trials, my journey was bigger and more significant than any temporary setback.

There's a choice in those moments when the world tempts you to snap, crackle, and pop under the weight of disappointment or injustice. Accountability is having people around you who remind you of the magnitude of your journey and the resilience that resides within. A loyal friend will say, "You have every right to be upset, but don't let a fleeting moment of anger unravel the tapestry of triumph you've woven."

When faced with wrongs committed against me, I found solace in restraint. People may not realize the wrongs they've done, for I chose not to react in the expected manner. Instead, I maintained my composure, treating them with kindness even when they least deserved it. It's a strategy that often leads them to distance themselves, realizing that their attempts to provoke a reaction were in vain.

In those challenging situations, I ask myself a vital question: What do I need to learn? Every person in the room is not in tune with the same frequency. Some may be a test, a challenge to see if I'll succumb to the allure of snapping under pressure. It's the crown-chakra moment—a test to determine if I will allow external circumstances to dislodge my sense of peace and self-control.

Acknowledging imperfection is an essential part of my journey. I proclaim it boldly: I am not perfect. Yet, in those moments when life slings challenges my way, I choose to respond with resilience, wisdom, and grace. I pull back, reassess, and ask tough questions about why a particular challenge is present in my life. Some days are undoubtedly hard, but in those moments, I draw strength from the understanding that each obstacle is a steppingstone to greater heights, a testament to the unyielding spirit within.

Cultivating unshakable self-worth requires testing. It comes not when everything flows perfectly but by leveraging turmoil to expand perspective and skills for the throne. How do we grow strong through trials rather than let them break us? This can be done by reframing our pain as purposeful.

Reframe Setbacks as Feedback

The first mental shift is to view each blow not as unjust punishment but essential feedback on strengthening our weak spots. Does an argument expose a trust gap needing repair? Does a rejection highlight skills requiring better demonstration of value? Spin the lens from victim to engaged student.

Write down constructive insights, even in unpleasant interactions. "Her leave revealed over-reliance on one person. Time to build community." This expands its capacity to attract support. Mine for gems in muck for rapid resilience building.

Leverage Challenges to Build Grit

Next, understanding unwanted change bears gifts of learning grit needed for long-term rule. Grit grows by bearing small daily frustrations with patient persistence rather than escaping all discomfort. Developing high tolerance for distress or delayed gratification conveys noble strength.

Use adversity as training grounds for overcoming greater obstacles ahead with flexibility. Bounce back after each bout stronger, wiser, more prepared to lead. Let little failures inoculate against catastrophe. Each one boosts resilience and self-trust far greater than constant smooth sailing!

Seek Support from Your Court

Finally, in hardship avoid isolation and instead allow trusted members of your court to uplift your spirits and faith. Even the mightiest monarchs temporarily lose sight of innate power when battered by storms. Your community offers a mirror of unshakable truth when your inner sight fails.

Collect affirmations of past victories and honorable character to drown out present challenges. Stay rooted in your divinely ordained capability to overcome but draw stability from soul companions during the passage. With deep faith in your resilience and ability to steer any storm, your tranquility will return.

My queens may these keys to royal resilience help you turn obstacles into opportunities! Never doubt your inner resolve and power to ascend stronger. Onward!

I want you to understand reframing and shifting your perspective how you can use it to help you. Reframing is a skill we can all strengthen with conscious practice over time. Here are a few tangible tips:

Start by noticing when your inner dialogue or feelings toward a challenge are coming from a "victim mentality" - full of blame on others/the world and helpless resignation. Write down those automatic thoughts.

Then purposefully shift perspective - ask yourself questions like:

- How might this be happening for me versus to me? What potential positive purposes could adversity serve?

- What strengths or lessons might I gain if I faced this head on? How might confronting this wisely make me more effective in the long-term?

- If I imagined myself as a queen/noble leader, how would I authoritatively steer through these rapids? What would make me more skillful?

Essentially talk to yourself with an empowered inner coach approach rather than a helpless victim. Speak about the situation and your ability to grow through it with charged language - "overcome" "leverage" "conquer".

Over time it rewires your neural pathways to automatically interpret difficulties as feedback for growth rather than existential threats stealing your inner peace. Be patient with yourself, it takes practice! But keep striving to reframe challenges as fuel for self-expansion and you'll cultivate grit fast.

ROYAL REVERENCE

Reframing mindfully ultimately builds unshakable confidence in overcoming anything while retaining grace.

Leveraging challenges to build grit is a mindset shift that takes practice but pays off in resilience long-term. Here's how to start:

The first step is getting comfortable with being uncomfortable. Rather than seeing inconvenience, delays, or exertion as awful burdens, reframe them as training grounds. Intentionally face small frustrations that present opportunity to expand your tolerance muscle.

For example, if you dislike chilly weather, bundle up and go for a brief winter walk anyway, noting it makes you tougher. Or if you avoid difficult conversations, speak briefly to less intimidating acquaintances first to build skills to have them with more challenging relationships.

Approach each irritation or dread as a chance to get 1% better at functioning during distress. Even diminutive activities repetitively over time develop grit and tenacity.

Also leverage bigger challenges that organically arise rather than circumvent them. If a work deadline requires hustle, put in longer hours even if unpleasant knowing you'll perform better under pressure next time. Use the opportunity as training versus complaining.

Essentially, the root of building grit is seeking difficulty rather than avoiding discomfort. It's a mentality grounded in confidence you can manage and grow from whatever arises, making you antifragile! Start by adding in small daily friction, you'd be amazed how your tolerance expands.

Seeking support when we feel afraid to be vulnerable is so vital yet takes courage to override old conditioning. Here are some thoughts:

First, remind yourself asking for help is never a weakness, but rather a sign of wisdom and self-awareness. All great leaders lean on others' strengths while focusing energy where they can personally excel. Assistance expands influence..

Remember too that your inner world shapes perception - when battered and exhausted by storms, vision narrows. Close confidants who remind you of bigger perspective and your timeless talents provide mirrors revealing wholeness obscured when caught in emotion. Let people hold hope on your behalf when yours wavers.

Start by just naming the emotions themselves to allies rather than details - "I'm feeling very scared and overwhelmed right now." Allow them simply to offer compassion, not necessarily solutions. Receive support through listening ear and shoulders to lean on without having to put on a brave face.

Then for those offering tangible reinforcement in areas of struggle, be explicit in asking for what formats uplift you - advice, advocacy, giving space for catharsis, sitting in supportive silence? Help them help you.

As resilience strengthens, intentionally pay your support forward too - our suffering containing collective purpose when lessons learned uplift others now struggling. Find meaning in the mountain climb through service on the descent.

You were never meant to rule alone - even seemingly solo climbs to summits depend on teams, guides, and community. What support might you request today?

A Royal Conclusion:

As we bring our time together to a close, my cherished rulers, I hope these lessons equipped you to meet obstacles as opportunities for self-expansion rather than existential threats to your inner peace or self-worth. Storms will continue arising, as change remains the only constant in our mortal realms. But through the tools of perspective shifting, grit development, and soul tribe reliance, you now contain invaluable resources to leverage turmoil for evolution into your highest sovereignty. Crown yourself with confidence in the promise of a brighter dawn no matter how long nights of the soul linger. And when rays peek again, reign over your domain with unmatched resilience, grace and vision uplifting your entire kingdom. Now go courageously, knowing storms only strengthen your right to rule!

Practical Exercise:

Over the next month, strengthen resilience through adversity with these steps:

1. Reframe 1-2 current setbacks as valuable feedback on areas for self-expansion. Ask, "How is this fortifying me?"

2. Intentionally face a small manageable discomfort that normally you avoid. Approach it as grit-building training.

3. Confide in a trusted member of your court about a challenge you feel afraid of sharing vulnerable feelings around. Allow them to comfort without solving.

4. Journal about an obstacle you recently overcame. Explore what that teaches you about your inner capability to manage turmoil.

Chapter 7 Noble Notable:

I cultivate deep confidence in my ability to overcome adversity by reframing difficulties as growth opportunities rather than threats, leveraging small daily frustrations to expand my resilience muscle, and relying on soul companions for support when temporarily losing my footing. Storms strengthen my right to rule.

It's your turn. How will you apply it? Write down what stuck out and how you'll apply it.

Reframe Current Setbacks:

1.

2.

3.

4.

5.

6.

7.

8.

9.

10.

Journal about an obstacle you overcame.

ROCHINDA PICKENS

ROYAL REVERENCE

A Closing Note on Royal Reverence

My esteemed community of noble rulers - we stand now at journey's end, having explored the intricate beauty of self-respect by way of queenly metaphors. What once appeared an unwieldy, lofty concept has unveiled step-by-step an eminently practical path to realizing our birthright royalty.

We cultivated unshakeable confidence not arrogance, moats of healthy boundaries not walls of isolation, courts of support not compromise, ruthless prioritization of nourishment understanding its ripple effects, and finally courage to wear crowns with pride, and not with apology.

Through it all, we found that true reverence starts as inward sight - not chasing validation but realizing every experience holds potential to polish self-worth's shining facets. Adversity bore gifts, if we but reframe challenges thus. Dark nights nourished wisdom if we seek encompassing perspective from soul companions. By learning to approve, appreciate and speak softly to ourselves first, external domains effortlessly transformed to reflect that luminous grace back.

I hope these humble offerings stirred recognition of the illimitable inner terrain awaiting your exploration. Rule justly over that landscape with utmost compassion and soon you'll witness outside kingdoms adopting similar shapes through sheer magnetic pull. Such is the alchemy of self-respect is fully embodied.

As your Crown Checker then, my concluding wish is simply this - let today's final page become the first steppingstone on the lifelong journey toward your own royalty. The path of fulfillment will solely overflow. Go rule with benevolence, beloveds! Our world sorely needs more awakened sovereigns...who reign.

Yours in service,
The Crown Checker

A Blessing on Your Journey

My beloved friends, as your guide The Crown Checker, what joy it has brought witnessing the unveiling of royalty within each of you through our travels together.

When we first met, the very notion of sacred self-respect bordered, or in fantasy for some. How could such divine birthrights have slipped?

But in truth, we dwell amidst a wounded culture of comparison stealing inherent worth away inch by inch until the shadows eclipse light. And misplacing crowns is no personal failing, it's simply the fog of our collective consciousness crying out for higher truth. The pendulum swings more and awakens us to reclaiming our majesty. We have to midwife our self-love back into existence - not through demanding pedestals, but patient nurturing of seeds already sown. We shined light on natural gifts awaiting appreciation. We nurtured our intrinsic courage and want validation. I sincerely hope these humble chapters stirred recognition of the sacred terrain residing within each soul no matter how deeply buried beneath our protective layers. For as we peel back those collective expectations and wounding, ultimately, we uncover perfection itself awaiting embrace. May you rule justly over that landscape with utmost benevolence, beloveds. The world sorely needs more enlightened sovereigns.

Don't stop owning the crown that belongs to you. It is YOURS!

~ Rochinda ~

About the Author

Rochinda Pickens is a life shift coach, motivational speaker, and best-selling author with a passion for guiding women who have made the empowering decision to live again. Rochinda's a wife, mother of three adult children, and a nana to three amazing grandchildren. She helps individuals who are embracing their breakdowns, while preparing for their breakthroughs.

After surviving a fatal car accident that profoundly altered the course of her life, Rochinda, a mother of three, found herself facing tough decisions, including the necessity of moving forward after her life literally shattered. Despite lacking a college degree or formal training, qualities often assumed to be possessed by successful entrepreneurs, she owned and operated Chinda's Younique Boutique for a decade.

During this time, Rochinda had the privilege of meeting incredible women from diverse backgrounds. It became clear to her that one of God's callings for her life was to demonstrate what intentional living entails. Renewed with a zest for life and fueled by the passion derived from sharing her story and aiding other women, she founded Kept Woman of God (KWOG), a 501c3 nonprofit organization connecting women globally through conferences, workshops, and retreats. These gatherings provide women the space to embrace their authenticity and share their voices, finding solace and empowerment in a community. Rochinda has also collaborated with individuals, both men and women, sharing their experiences and struggles through book collaborations, guided by divine inspiration.

Through Rochinda's journey, she has broken through barriers and now endeavors to pass on her hard-earned wisdom to others, guiding them through the process of starting over and equipping them for success. Her latest venture, Chinda and Friends, an eCommerce business promoting clean living, is a testament to her ongoing commitment to being a beacon of hope for others. Reflecting her inclusive philosophy, the company's motto is, "Everyone who enters the door - come in as friends, but hang around long enough, and you become family."

Rochinda's signature talk, "Finding Joy in the Journey: Choosing to Live Intentionally," encapsulates her philosophy of embracing life with purpose and gratitude. A member of the Sister Circle of Greater Kansas City and a three-time national best-selling author, she has also created the program

"**Write with Chinda,**" empowering women and men to share their stories and become published authors. Her famous phrase, "It's not a minute, moment, or weekend. It's a lifestyle," encapsulates her belief in the transformative power of intentional living.

Join Rochinda for a **Chosen Luxury Experience** which provides the Queens that you are with a special escape from the day to day & enjoy some beautiful, self-care, just for you. Each experience is carefully curated with the Queen in mind. You can find out more and get updates at ChosenLuxuryExperience.com. The details are shared in a Buy One, Bless One format to enable you and a bestie to come together, or if you're a solo traveler who is ready to relax on their own and meet a few new acquaintances, you will not be disappointed.

KWOG Ambassadors are another way to join us by helping other women embrace their noble selves. You ask, what is a "KWOG Ambassador"? She's a sister who serves. A sister who links arms and ensures her sister's crown stays upright on her head, in her heart, and by her hand. These are the women who help us share the mission of the conference each year. We are women-kept by God, not ourselves. The Lord provides us with the tools, resources, and other women to help us.

Every year we are growing and building women up in their faith, finances, and their futures. No woman is left behind. You can help by sharing the conference and pledging to bring 10 sisters with you to be encouraged, motivated and built up. We host an Ambassadors meet & greet, share ways to help us grow, share perks of the program and are looking forward to serving one million sisters by 2050. Will you join us? If you would be interested, email us at staff@keptwomanofgod.com.

More Works from Rochinda Pickens

- From Being Kept to Being Kept
- Picking Up the Pieces
- The Life I Love
- Seeds of Hope
- The I'm Chosen Journal

Available at www.Rochinda.com

WE WANT TO HEAR FROM YOU

If this book has made a difference in your life Rochinda would be excited to hear about it.

Please leave a review on Amazon.com

Book Rochinda to speak at your next event.
Send email to staff@KeptwomanofGod.com

BOOK ROCHINDA

www.ingramcontent.com/pod-product-compliance
Lightning Source LLC
Chambersburg PA
CBHW070303230426
43664CB00014B/2621